Yet Life was a Triumph

Yet Life was a Triumph

POEMS AND MEDITATIONS

Sharon M. Carr

Preface by James T. Laney
President, Emory University

A Division of Thomas Nelson Publishers

NASHVILLE

Published in Nashville, Tennessee, by Oliver-Nelson Books, a division of Thomas Nelson, Inc., Publishers, and distributed in Canada by Lawson Falle, Ltd., Cambridge, Ontario.

Printed in the United States of America.

Library of Congress Cataloging-in-Publication Data

Carr, Sharon, 1967–1990.
Yet life was a triumph : poems and meditations / Sharon Carr.
p. cm.
ISBN 0-8407-9595-5 (hardcover)
I. Title.
PS3553.A76336Y48 1991
811′.54—dc20 91–7178
CIP

2 3 4 5 6 — 96 95 94 93 92 91

Contents

GRIEF

ANGER

Preface

Despite an all-too-brief life, Sharon Carr left a remarkable and enduring legacy. Stricken by a brain tumor in her youthful prime, her few remaining years were consumed in a struggle with death and an attempt to understand God's will. That her spirit did not break under the terrible certainty of an early death is a triumph. That it achieved self-transcendence through poetic expression is an inspiration.

One need make no concession to youth or sentimentality when reading her poems and meditations. They portray how she probed deeper and deeper into her faith, distilling it from easy consolation and seductive distraction. The result was a faith tested under the most exacting circumstances, expressed with moving and heartrending power. Her explorations of the soul are severe, austere, and chaste. None of us can accompany her without being chastened in the truest sense—made purer, more reflective, more spiritually alive. Her life, though tantalizingly brief, left an enduring legacy, a noble legacy. We are all her spiritual debtors.

James T. Laney
President, Emory University

Foreword

The lack of fulfillment in individual human beings is a major subject in the poems of John Crowe Ransom. His characters often fail to develop their souls because of early death, lack of physical and sexual development and power, or excessive intellectuality at the expense of the body or the emotions. Many of his poems are about the old conflict between the body and the soul.

In my course on Southern literature at Emory University in the spring of 1987, I began as I usually did with the poems of John Crowe Ransom. "Janet Waking," a poem about a little girl's realization of the meaning of death when her pet hen dies, and "Bells for John Whiteside's Daughter," a poem about the death of a little girl, were two of the earliest ones I taught. When that class was over—I did not yet know the names of my students—an attractive, dignified, red-haired young woman walked into my office and said, "I am a dying child."

"What do you mean?" I asked.

"I have had two operations for tumors of the brain, and the treatments since then have not stopped the growth of the cancer," she said. "I have to have other treatments and probably other operations." That was my first acquaintance with Sharon Carr.

With all her troubles, Sharon made the A we both expected in the course, and we did not discuss her troubles a great deal. It did not seem there was much to say beyond the usual talk and discussion of sensitive and great works of literature. When the class went on a picnic to my farm, Sharon was one of the group, but there was no discussion of cancer. So far as I knew, few were aware that she was afflicted. We were close as student and teacher and persons, but not as the well and the sick.

The next fall I checked to see if Sharon had returned to school. She had. So I checked no more. Often I wondered what had happened, but somehow it seemed a little too personal to inquire or investigate.

Just before Christmas in 1988 I received a collection of poems and meditations, including nearly all of those published here. It was bound in a green notebook cover, with the poems photocopied on both sides of the pages. A kind of kindergarten scrawl had awkwardly printed *S H A R O N* across the bottom of the cover.

Inside, in the handwriting of her mother, Ruth Carr, Sharon said that she had had to drop out of school, that she had had more operations, that one cyst of the brain had continued constantly to drain, that she had written some poems and meditations and wished to share them with a few of her friends.

Most student poems are a burden in the life of a teacher of literature, and I opened the book drearily and began to read. One poem drove me to the next. I found myself reading the best poetry I had ever read by any college student. The sensitivity, the poetic skill, the range of learning, the spiritual depth, far excelled the work, I believed, of many accomplished and publishing poets.

Sharon had been pursuing a double major in English and Religion. She had a 3.9 average on a 4.0 basis. She was a National Merit Scholar and would have been a Bobby Jones Scholar in an exchange program with Saint Andrews University in Scotland if she had not had to drop out of school in the first term of her junior year because of the troubles with cancer.

I remembered that Emory University years before had

awarded posthumously a Master of Science degree to a young man in Chemistry, and his wife had walked across the graduation stage and received the diploma in his name. The departments of English and Religion agreed to recommend to the Dean of Emory College that Sharon Carr be given an honorary Bachelor of Arts degree. Reasoning that she had completed the two-year residency requirement, that she had an extraordinarily high level of academic accomplishment, and that the book of poems showed more than the learning of the usual holder of a bachelor's degree, Dean David Minter and President James Laney carried the recommendation to Emory's Board of Trustees. The president read some of Sharon's poems to the trustees. Some wept. Unanimously, they voted to award Sharon the degree of Bachelor of Arts, earned rather than honorary.

Because of fears that Sharon might be unable to attend the graduation ceremonies later, President Laney and Dean Minter journeyed to Augusta, Georgia, where Sharon and her family lived, and presented her diploma in a small ceremony. But in May 1989, Sharon, her family, and I sat in the front row at Emory's commencement. Sharon sat in a wheelchair, and the dean graciously brought the diploma down to her where she sat. She graduated, as a Dean's Scholar, with her class.

At lunch that graduation day, although she could not feed herself, Sharon laughed with her usual gusto and talked with strength and wisdom. She showed—as her poems do—her deep love of God and her astonishing lack of self-pity.

In the year and a half of life that remained to her, she worked with several of us at Emory to prepare this book for publication. All of us who knew Sharon Carr in person are glad that many others will come to know her in her poems: her joy in life, her trust in God, her fulfillment of spirit in the face of death.

Few people at the age of nineteen are put in the position of composing their own epitaph, as Sharon was when she wrote the poem of that title placed at the end of this volume. There are even fewer who would conclude it as Sharon did:

> Because I was forced to live life boldly,
> thankfully,
> lovingly and
> joyfully,
> death is tender,
> and life was a triumph.

This poem was read at her funeral, a "Service of Witness to the Resurrection and Thanksgiving for the Life of Sharon Michele Carr," at Covenant Presbyterian Church in Augusta, Georgia, on October 3, 1990.

Floyd C. Watkins
Charles Howard Candler Professor
of American Literature, Emeritus
Emory University

Yet Life was a Triumph

POEMS AND MEDITATIONS

Sharon M. Carr

Bewilderment

Spring 1984 *through Summer* 1985

Letter to a Climber

Echoes of goodbye ring in my fingers
as I touch each letter of your lonely
name. . . . .
My eyes are bluer
for the tears I've given you,
and my tense veined hands are softer in
the
strumming of your picture;
There is lament in counting
the black mountain pinnacles that stand static
as we whirl by,
and rejoicing in the valleys
we have survived.
In those red-mud canyons
the goodbyes find a voice
and are immortalized in waves of
unending sound. . . . .
I am remembering the range, loved one,
and the rope around my waist is stronger
because you pulled it taut when you left the
summit,
never to hit the ground.

Cancer

You
did not understand when a part of me
died;
You
did not believe that death threatens
my doorstep every day;
You
could not comprehend that I had been violated,
ravished, roped and tied——
You
neglected to accept that my malignancy was alive,
throbbing, intrinsically my own. . . . .
And you
forgot to hold a funeral for the undaunted hero
inside me
struck from the sky with unwavering arrow.

Sickness

Hovering storm
fleeting——
Shocks of lightning intertwine with the
ebony ribbons of sad sky;
Tomorrow is another day,
said Scarlett,
and colored water dapples the fountain. . . . .
Light games imprison the lonely branch——
a storm is coming,
And I am waiting for the
lightning
to crack the security. . . . .
No chance——
oak bone rattles with hollow feeling,
and lies remembered.
It's still there, in my heart——
I have no reason to be mangled
by rain. . . . .
and lies remembered.

Daily Bread

Open your mouth and eat,
for the night is over
and the grafting begins. . . . .
Repressed pictures gurgling in my dreams,
skull-dashing, flesh-tearing
sheets soaked in blood;
The metal darkness was so heavy,
screwing tighter into my cheeks,
bolting hard above my spine——
it's over.
Still my soul, Elohim,
and teach me again
to take the food You give me
with gladness——
This is the day the Lord hath made.
Rejoice.

Evangelism

There it was,
staring me in the face,
in your eyes. . . . .
I felt trapped, confronted, touched
with the quiet power that had created
galaxies and brought to dust space kingdoms;
There it was,
in your wise words,
your gentle touch,
your pure laugh——
not many of us can laugh simply for the sake
of mirth, joyful and with thanksgiving. . . . .
There it was,
in the simple gesture of extending your hand
for mine, to care and to listen.
In you,
my loving friend,
is the God-image,
Alive and
Beautiful and
Refreshing——
Thank you for sharing, and allowing me to glimpse
the brightness of Christ's kingdom
through the mirth
in your eyes.

SC

The Promise

Chasing the sunrise,
delicious in the electric henna and soft mulberry bath,
I cherished the silence.
The raucous laughter of a hundred evenings was vile
in this temple of morning——
Coarse creatures that we are;
My mind longed to speak, anxious to share the miracle,
but my heart refused sound.
Speak to me, I begged the glowing curls of light,
instill in me your wisdom.
Ah, my sun-child,
conceived in darkness, raised in dusk,
we witness different worlds:
I bring color and serenity and wakefulness to the people-harbor,
but you thrash to keep from drowning.
I am the mark of a new beginning,
while you struggle to shake off the old.
I take nothing, for I have no need,
and you are not willing to give everything,
for you mistrust the certainty that your place
in the plan is secure.
We are one only in the name of beauty——
You hunger,
I satisfy.
Peace I leave with you,
that on cloudy days,
you are assured
I will rise.

Your Hand Lifts Me

In the swirling waters of sorrow and suffering, You beckoned me come——I needed to walk where You had walked, to know Your steps. But You are merciful, and spared me the Golgothan pilgrimage. . . . . Betwixt the batter of wind and sea, my being began to sink, and I was made afraid. I now know the doubt, and the fear and the humility of the walk on holy water——I also know it is Your hand that lifts me from a watery grave.

I Am Willing

1 Samuel 3

My will bends, Father, in the softening of Your strong hands, and I am ready to engrave in stone the principles of Your service, the stone of my reality. . . . . Your voice is so often mistaken for the beckoning of a man-master, and it is in this allegiance we lose our life to the prince of darkness; Still You call, still You speak, still You lend hard messages of living to grate upon our lips——
I am willing. Grasp my stone for Your dwelling:
Speak, Lord, for Thy servant hears.

Fall 1985

She Didn't Wipe the Tear

She didn't wipe the tear away. It fell weakly,
like the crumpled leaf after torrential wind;
It carved a vermillion gutter into her face,
burning, torching, rending
the visage of assurance, until the true features
belched forth——
she never lifted a finger to hide her shame.
Misshapen skull of humanity,
your poison has made tear ducts obsolete,
without a proper place for memories to
fall. . . . .
In our scramble to mask over the honesty of sorrow,
we forgo crying honestly.

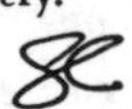

Portrait of a Goose

Just a little farther now, stolid duck statues,
and the ripple you are bound to will meet the
shore;
Black marbles for eyes, rimmed in orange,
like tears in effigy——having no need to
weep.
Your waddle makes me think you have no hip,
clop, clop, water-plop——
Brain cleft making me straggle along unjointed,
eternally searching for a familiar pond to tread
in.
If you pinched the arcs of ductile web together,
your steps would be even——
but then it would be impossible
to swim.

SC

Seedling

Candle glow a fortress against the frost,
refusing the indistinction of blank whiteness,
needing to burn the hoary conformity of
winter
until a niche would house its light. . . . .
The sky it calls to hovers in amber immobility,
like the ear of God pressed tightly to His earth, slit
barely
for the moon's cumbersome comment——
listening
intensely for each contraction of the seed sheathed in soil;
It is flickering too, seeking significance
in the uncomplicated courage of growth,
resting in His warm attention while
allowing a fetal soul
to burn the frost and uncurl petals
to the world below its window.

ICU Chatter

Wet silver darkness,
you are my only companion,
and though you are no friend, I welcome your even touch. . . . .
Sometimes you inspire fear,
sometimes anger,
necessity spawning faith;
The granules of your shroud play hide and seek
with my eyes, darting and disappearing
into your protective nestle.
I'd like to believe you
when you say 'I am reality and this
is the only love there is.'
I'd like to stay covered,
hidden from the ache of seeing things
as they really are. . . . .
Companion darkness,
you will suffice for my wounded retreat,
but I much prefer
the healing truth of facing light-enlivened
day.

Torn, to Be Healed

He has torn that He may heal us, and we are stricken, but our faithful Lord will bind us up; So many deaths to suffer, so many people afraid of their bodies and the death that body keeps. . . . .
I will not let them punish me for being torn, and always will I press on to know the Lord——and His healing.

The Child in Us

The child in us never allows the self to be violated, because she knows we do not belong to ourselves, and we are worth saving; The child in us is determined and dedicated to finding Truth, because she knows instinctively that Truth is light, and light is good; Eventually we learn to hammer out this trust, because we are afraid of not having someone to belong to——not even ourselves. And thus we push away what was worth saving, and we die terrified, meaningless deaths——Let God revive the child in you. . . . . He makes a world of difference when you're dying.

I Have to Learn

The time is at hand, the season of killing, plucking up. I can feel the breath of death close on my neck, demanding the thought process I value so much. . . . . And so I learn——rapidly, roaringly, open-eyed and hungry; I have to learn, because someday I want to teach those You entrust to me how to follow. . . . . You, precious Christ, You. Dying is not so omnipresent, so destructive anymore. My day will come, and I will fill my time with learning about You and me and Your work in me, open-eyed and hungry.

How Do You Say?

How can we say the Christ is not relevant, or lives on an abstract plane we cannot broach? Indeed, His visions are those we could never imagine, and His joy-sadness is a mixture unfathomable to our rigid minds. . . . . How can we say our Wonderful Counselor knows not our slavery when He Himself took our feet, washing and toweling with His tears our bleeding sores; How can we say He is not Lord when in His service to us, He resolved a prophet's dreams and erased the curse of our sins before His Father? His love and His example are unsurpassed——

How do you say?

You Said Let Go

You said let go, live in the giggles of light and, for even a moment, ignore the consuming bellows of blackness. I tried that one time. And I enjoyed myself so much I died all over again upon returning to reality.

Winter 1985

Deplorare Alius

Belches of living fire spring from the mouths of babes,
and curdle on the tongues of the lonely. . . . .
You could not cry with me,
so I choke on the soul-wrenching
sobs——
Your pain is not my pain.
You could not face the awkward moment,
so you hid when I called your name——
Your sorrow is not my sorrow.
You did not have the words to give my eulogy,
so my ashes were splattered on the sea without
remembrance——
Your death is not my death.
You would not hold my maimed hand,
so I was deprived of touch.
Your grief is not my grief.
Brother Cain, my blood is in the soil,
and I will reap long after
your arid lands leave you starving.

Biologically Speaking

They opened up my head
to see what they could see,
but the only monster they found
was a tiny gleaming tooth,
white and serrated among the grainy gray
cells;
My brain sighed,
and the hard spot yielded to the
gush
of fluid cleansing, cleansing.
And then I was dead——
but still I walk and talk,
for souls are very stubborn,
and their wellspring of life
does not issue
from mere tissue.

Courage . . . Suffering Soldier

The danger is heaving blasts of fear against me, and the constant threat wearies me; The stairsteps are growing steeper and steeper, and secure footing is harder to sustain. . . . . And then You call out to me—— Courage and Trust, suffering soldier, in the unflinching railing that is always within your desperate grasp.

Receive the Spirit

You breathed on our feeble bodies the wind of comfort; You spoke softly the Counselor of our days, a shaft of light in the cold gray mornings of our separation. . . . . You appeared to our grief-sick reality bringing a gift from the Father, a hope and a joy in the blisters of trial——Receive the Spirit. With an empty life, O my Lord, will I gladly receive.

Grief

Spring 1986

Messiah

Lonely air oozes through the flaking window seal,
and I smell hopelessness.
Shriveled plaster crinkles in the antiseptic stench,
and I sweat horror.
Snarling machines open their jaws to break me,
and the intercourse with pain
begins;
I labor in the desert,
the forsaken valley of life half-empty
and death half-full. . . . .
I know You are here, Emmanuel,
for every once in a while the red tide
recedes, and
the light of Your smile shines blue;
I know You are in agony, Hashem,
and out of love Your bruised wounds lie
bare. . . . .
You came to me in my loneliness,
in the Cross of Your Son.

The Marys, the Master, and Me

A baby is born——a woman cries.
In the beginning there were no tears. . . . .
When the first muscle molded motion, when the first joint protruded
with knobby head, when brain cells sparked
in their first impulse——You were there.
Your chest heaved with the tide of Life even as ours did,
for You were the first-born who witnessed the first birth;
Even then You knew Your Father's mind and bent to Your Father's will,
for You were the Word which was the language of our being. . . . .
And when self was idolized and fought to control even its Maker,
once again You obeyed and sought to reach us through the womb;
The Lord is crucified——a woman cries.
Tomorrow I might die——
Hope is alive.

Terminal Youth

You were my sister, and now you're gone.
The disease grew bigger than you,
pronouncing
an edict of death——however loud it
screeched,
your laugh tingled louder,
filling bleeding ears with balm, lighting
candles
with the oil of tenuous hope. . . . .
You were my friend,
and you deserted me.
The words we shared are the text of my every
thought,
the grace and peace that bound us together
fragmented;
You were my daughter, and we never said goodbye.
The fruit of my loin, the endowment that
ensures
tomorrow——dead.
You are all of these,
and a Child of God——
His creation, His thought.
Tomorrow is another day
for the people you left behind,
and a lifetime's not too long
to keep the candles
lit.

With Hind's Feet

My body is trembling,
rottenness seethes in my bones,
and the flock is cut off from the fold;
The scars across my head
are stinging as Thy wrath
against the rivers, and I am weary
of being the rag-doll amidst beauty,
stitched together because she fell apart. . . . .
I am waiting for the day of trouble,
the day when my puppet parts no
longer
have to be prodded, and I can dance with
You.
The fig tree hath no blossom,
Lord,
and the final fruit has fallen from the
vine——
only the rag-doll has reason to rejoice,
for there will be dancing
upon the high places.

Come By Here

The tender reed is bruised,
the sculptured cheekbone smashed
by drills of fear——
Kum ba yah.
River dross is drowning life,
choking the newborn hope it brings
to the forlorn valley——
Kum ba yah.
Magnolia trees are birthing buds that sit high
on borrowed dignity like cream baubles
on lonely debutantes, decorated but soon to
wither. . . . .
Kum ba yah.
The tears of tomorrow have come today,
and I weep as often as I pray——
Kum ba yah.
The burnt offerings please You no more, my Lord,
and obedience means following when there is no
light,
listening when no voice peals,
dying when we see no glory,
and praying even as we weep. . . . .
Kum ba yah.

Woods Behind the Hospital

Under your umber awning
                        the mud-splash breeze tells of
            the rain and the sod-stink
                        it left behind——
            a brief, lukewarm lure
of surface smells, never watering deep enough
                                        to open the molasses earth;

Have I come here to die?
            a navy-tailed bird inspires me
                        to cry, the uncomely weather-twisted trunk
                                        a mirror of the sigh
                        too deep for words, praying when we
                        cannot. . . . .
I rest in your shade, scarred one,
                        and the rain did last long enough
            to make me dig
                                                for deeper earth.

Once Forsook, Now Understood

Waiting to die,
drinking deep the draught of suffering,
wringing every moment until a reason to trudge on
drips sullenly forth;
Watching the flower
bend and break as the careless heel of
affliction
crushes its abundance of vitality, and beauty, and
color,
until its place knows it no more. . . . .
Biding the halcyon hill,
the point of departure,
the place where humanity faced
forsakenness——
My God, my God, why hast Thou. . . . . restored
us?
Hope and Horror are the beams
that cross in the middle——
You hung there,
that I may drink deeply of Life.

Already Praying

I asked you to pray for me——
the suffering has begun, and the skull-wracking pain
is a shadow I know only too well. . . . .
I wanted you to console me,
for the breadth of my grief gnashes at me with steely
teeth, hacking and clawing at my shreds of hope,
and stubborn strands of faith;
And then you told me Jesus
prays for me,
that He pleads with His Father on my behalf,
that the strength of the Cross sustains me. . . . .
The tears are rolling from both our faces, friend——
Let me comfort you,
for Someone in heaven has already
comforted me.

The Alpha in the Omega

i

We shower You with palms, great Lord, for we know not what You will require
of us. . . . .
The sun burnishes the green leafy edges,
and the smooth oil-sheen is sticky——
not unlike our shriveled faith in the heat of trial. . . . .
I hear the jubilation of those watching the gate, and soon Your royal garments
will ruffle the dust before me,
and I will whisper 'Hosanna';
You will pass into our city, and the reign of men must bow down and worship
their new King——how often we have fit reality into
our need for joy. . . . .
Divine Jesus,
You rode in only one parade here in Your kingdom,
and for a carriage we gave You an ass,
for loyalty we waved spineless palms,
and for obedience we delivered You up——
unto death.
You needed not our pitiful allegiance,
but accepted even our Cross,
that we should encounter the courage and compassion
of our God-King.

ii

The grail at Your lips
is hot with shame, holding the wine of our iniquity,
the blood of our transgressions;

The supple loaf in Your hands is cowering in anticipation of being broken——
wrenched and consumed by our insatiable hunger, even as our self-deceptions
led You to the tearing of tissue and bone,
stretched across a grieving sky. . . . .
The light in Your eyes is sculpting a vision in the stone of history,
gleaning guilt from suffering,
threshing hope from the womb of tragedy;
The hand that dips in the dish of humanity
awaits the claw of betrayal,
greedy fingers slicing at sinless skin,
smearing covenant blood across the loins of the Lamb——
Is it I, Master?

iii

The very stones are crying out,
their organic voices wailing as we become their brothers
in inhumanity. . . . .
The ninth hour is upon us,
and it is finished.
We have scorned for the last time Yahweh's lesson, the mercy of His
outstretched arms——a man hung dying in the rain. . . . .
We have defiled and dethroned the sovereignty of the King above kings
at the final curtain——now it is shred in two;
From the ashes of our cowardly crucifixion, the phoenix of redemption will fly,
the harbinger of freedom resurrected.
From the broken tomorrows of lives so much more unworthy than His,
the eternal Morning begins.

You followed Him,
You betrayed His trust,
You denied your holy fellowship with Him,
and you pierced His side to watch the blood and water mingle while
you laughed. . . . .
But His legs were not broken.
He looked upon you, and through His pain He forgave you.
And me.
Forever.
He bowed His head and gave up His spirit——so must we.
Hear these my prayers, O true King,
and with head hung low I offer this,
my spirit.

iv

Little lily throttled by the weight of this stone,
your comforting scent strangled by our heaviness,
our obsession for sealing off our guilt. . . . .
I came here to vent my desolation,
to mourn the kingdom that was to come,
to weep.
I came to ask Why,
and to tell this deaf-dumb tomb
the dew of hope has evaporated even as the vinegar on my King's lips
grew cold at the kiss of death;
Little lily,
why did we hurt you?
The pestle of self-possession has ground your soft membranes
into chalky dust,
the powder of our funeral pyre;

Little lily,

where did they hide my Jesus?
Did heaven take Him up to lead the royal
train as it sweeps the
universal chasms, the long tresses a
healing stroke on the raw wounds
of our creaturehood?
Tell me, lily——
Tell me where the Christ has gone.

v

Crackle, flash——the synapse is complete.
Lightning has soldered heaven with earth,
and the new order is announced in the
thunder. . . . .
An angel alights.
The words he carries are the ones
we are sent to proclaim——
Why do you seek the living among the
dead?
He is risen;
With blanched raiment,
the global portals quaking at the
import
of the Son's travail,
We hear once again the victory speech
wrenched from agony at Calvary——
He Is Risen
†††
The napkin of death lies crumpled in the corner of our
forsaken pain,
and the linen cloths of self-reliance have
been rolled up
by holy hands, sealing what the angel
said——
Seek not the living among the dead.

vi

The black wound of the empty tomb
reminds me of hurting in the darkness
because You have left me,
withdrawing into the silence of Your
loneliness. . . . .
The terror is gnawing at me, challenging me, destroying me;
I'm coming closer, Lord, to touch the
deadness of Your body,
the deadness of my distraught
emotion.
Where are You, Lord?
Can the tales be true?
Have You risen???
Suddenly Your absence in the death chamber
becomes the anomaly of vibrant Life, the
quieting of my fear,
the Victory!!!!!!
Sing Alleluia to the Lord!!
He is alive!
The darkness of my pain has not overcome the Light——
He will shine forever.
Yes, the tomb is empty. . . . .
Death, where is thy sting?

vii

The pungent dust clouds my vision,
irritating my eyes, lodging in my throat,
afflicting the
grooves of my fingers with sticky
film. . . . .
The dust of our sadness makes us still, unwilling to fight the
slander
of a Lord we hoped would redeem Israel;
Yet, we trudge on, nursing flickers of hope that the rumors
are true. . . . .
Emmaus, your distance is too great.

We travel to find refuge,
to sift the many grains of our sorrow,
to escape the searing poignancy
of our pain. . . . .
The prospect of living without You has finally stabbed the flimsy
cellophane of consciousness,
and I am bleeding water. . . . .
My whimpering spirit is tight with grief, and my face is like flint——
We are so tired, Lord.
The last trumpet of a mortal universe has sounded,
and we hear the voice of a man——
Who is this you are speaking of?
Why does Jerusalem lie in mourning as a mother whose first-born
has been wrenched from the womb only to breathe first the
stale air of death?
We cannot believe his heart is unscathed by the event that will change
time and history irrevocably and like no other;
We cannot fathom the bliss of his simple curiosity or the depth of
his ignorance. . . . . We walk with him.
We tell him who our King was——the first proclamation of good news,
though we knew it not.
In great understanding, this man penetrated our hazy vision with his words——
Was it not necessary the Christ should suffer?
Did He not enter His glory as a Lord intimate with the pain
of humanity, now more worthy of compassion and mercy
because He knew creature as well as Creator?

Enthralled, we ask him to stay and break bread with us——
the bittersweet irony of the broken loaf. . . . .
And suddenly, after thanking and blessing, our eyes were opened;
Amidst the torment of our journey, He had walked with us.
Among the vestiges of broken hearts, He was present.
Alongside the bereaved, confused hurt of our escape,
He followed us.
Praise be to God——
our Lord appears when the dust grows thickest,
when the sorrow crushes our courage,
when we are blind.
If we listen,
if we witness,
if we take Him into our homes and our hearts,
He will open our eyes.
. . . .
What I have written I have written.
Amen.

Comrade

The world cracked my helmet, Lord, and cut it off. . . . .
O my hope of salvation;
The world pried off my breastplate, Father,
and dug in my chest until it was sure
everything
was gone——faith and love, that is;
The world divided my feet in two,
shaving my bones and gouging out Your gospel
of peace——
Why do You leave me alone?
Brother Job, I share your bewilderment and your wretched pain,
but between your time and mine
there stands one difference——
my friends came
to build me up in encouragement
for Lord Jesus died to make it so. . . . .
They shall ride as warriors wielding the sword of the Spirit——
and each piece of me
will live
in all of them.

Ascension

Jesus, rest Your weary head upon my hands,
hands tainted with blood of my sin, of the thorn
entrenched in Your blessed brow. . . . .
Jesus, stretch Your arms across my back,
that I may know in a small way the heaviness of
Your burden;
Jesus, place Your feet on my knees, and let their
wrenching pain ease my shame and
stir my compassion——
Dear sweet Christ,
rest Your head on my grave,
that I may ascend with You
to life.

The Real Teacher

Right in the middle of class, amidst our lecture bugaboo, You propped Yourself against the podium, and watched. Your face was the gentle curve of sunlight, and Your angular body like the double-edged sword cutting to the marrow; But more pervasive than Your actual presence was the intent with which You looked and listened. Wisely, vigorously, peacefully You watched us, guiding with Your eyes our learning. Keep being the real teacher, Jesus, with the world as Your classroom.

Baptized into Jesus
Romans 6:3–4

Baptized into death with You, Jesus, walking the road with a cross, anticipating the untarnished crown. . . . . Buried with You, my Lord, heavy soil packing me in, blocking breath from nostril, gritty on the tongue, dark. Your own people raped Your brow with thorns, and bartered for the only scraps of Your human dignity; Still, Your beauty rose above all men, and every ounce of Your blood was mirrored in Your Father's tears. . . . .
Raised with You, King Jesus Christ, into newness of life.

I Washed Your Feet

I washed your feet so you would know my knee was bent in love, and my shoulders were hunched because I wanted to give, even as I had been given to. . . . . I wanted to learn humility, to serve even in pain, to say goodbye; I didn't know how much longer I would have to bear this burden, and I wanted to make my promise to meet you again in eternity without question——
I washed your feet because Jesus first washed mine.

Bought Anew

Wash my feet, Lord, for I am dirty; My sin has stained the snowy fleece of Your stamp on me——I am unworthy. Wrap my head in soft linen, Lord, for I am dying. . . . . The canker grows day by day, eating, eating, eating away; Cradle me in the loving sanctity of Your arm, Lord, for I am tired. The bristle of my bittersweet journey is wearing me down, thorny crown. Give me Your feet, Lord, and let me rinse them with my hair, for I am bought anew.

Human Baubles

Here they are——the gutting, galling sorrow, tormenting fear of being alone when I die, the butterflies of seeing Your face and touching it. . . . . Here they are, my human baubles. I've come to leave them at Your cross because You will make them new. And You will wear them around Your feet. I've set them down, Lord. Teach me to turn and leave them.

We Exchange Yokes

I barely have the strength to pray, bending on weary knee, not having words to shape what my heart aches to say. . . . . My distraught head hangs in weakness, bullets of pain piercing all endurance; And then You draw near to me, Jesus, the strength of Your eyes helping me see in my blindness, the strength of Your arm supporting my floundering head limp with sickness. . . . . I had only to whisper, and the rock-strong grace of Your Father brought You to me——we exchange yokes.

My Beginning and End

Alpha and Omega of my faith, let me believe forever. . . . . All I can see in the quotient of my consciousness is a puddle of blood, a skull divided; The cancer cleaves at the talents You gave me—— I want only to multiply them, but disease buries them with stagnation. . . . . You are my beginning and You are my end——Help me believe until then.

One Needy Sheep

My all-consuming need for reassurance is fed——I am the door. I lay down My life for the sheep. My emptiness is knocking——You are strapped to a tree in answer. . . . . I am weeping alone——wrenched from Your lips the agony of forsakenness; I am so afraid——Your touch is mercy, and Your promise is forgiveness. . . . . I am but one sheep, and You gave Your life that I might have life, and have it abundantly.

Holy Week

The holy days are passing, and Christ prepares once again to weep for Jerusalem, to make the trek to Golgotha. . . . . It is Holy Week, and I am dying. My humanity is desecrating my hope in life, and I am looking for another Way, the third Day. You embody my anguish, sweet Jesus, and for Your unselfish sake the Father will abolish death; It is Holy Week, and You are dying.

Your Vision

The darkness is not dark to You, and blindness cannot overcome You with sightlessness. . . . . Your vision burns in me, Lord, teaching me to see without eyes and touch without fingers——I may lose these very wits, Father, but even without eyes I will weep, and even without the ability of fingers, I will touch them with Your vision.

Summer 1986

The Tie That Binds

Weeping that will not come
                    thuds on Plexiglas eyes,
              smudging those pictures of loving
              and loved Magi bringing myrrh
                    to the messenger of Life. . . . .
Primal torrents of the human frustration
              slosh in my cavities of sight——
                    a heart bewildered by the horizontal rain;
You are but one friend,
                    and you manage to see
                    all my hidden tears
    while I wait
              for the cunning bow to glisten
                    upon my cracked cheek.
We cry out to death,
              not being heard,
                    and only when we touch the bloody tear
                    the messenger wears
    can we release our humanity
              with the sorrow that leaves us
                          real.

Don't Go Down

The water weaves gold
and a delicious shiver marks
the descent
of evening;
The wind ceases its toil,
tethered in the liquid coil of each
estuarine ripple——
Stillness absolves the sins
of zealous movement, lending peace to what
was merely brutal hope. . . . .
And on the breathless bank enshrined by the heart of God,
my kinship with the setting sun rankles
where once sorrow was only a vagabond——
now in hostel residence.
Overgrown peach of our solar system,
the pit of grief you entomb
forgives faster
than hope.

Invitation

Oyster shells clucking,
the bony sand cracking crisply
beneath my feet
as the sky wrinkles into a tight-lipped
smirk. . . . .
Bubblegum-textured foam
crackles soundlessly atop my toes
like bubbles of fat on bacon, nasty when they
pop;
The graceful tide attempts a gesture of friendship,
curling around my ankles with a vanilla
milkshake chill——
You have a higher calling, sea-ferret,
and whatever promises I might give you in return
would not ebb back to me.

To the Master

Master Sufferer, we adore Thee.
You bear the arrows of my evil in Your back,
anchored in the whip tracks. . . . .
You swirl with me in the sarabande of confusion,
upholding my limp limbs as we laugh in the heavenly chasms;
Triumphant Victor, we adore Thee.
The parade we marched You in cannot compare
to the glory You now receive, the might of Your God-given kingdom. . . . .
You wear the shame of my degradation
in the spittle on Your Father-kissed cheeks,
pretending to be tears but never cleansing
the socket-sore sorrow as tears should. . . . .
You shoulder disease, and death, and fear, and alienation
and the brutality of sin in the crown
adorning Your anointed head;
We cannot know the utter sadness and undeserved agony
of Your bitter cup, but we can taste Your potion——
God who died
that I might not wither away in pain
and fail to love even my life of sickness,
I adore
Thee.

SK

Reprieve from Summer

Twilight mercy
Shines without scorching, shadowbox
liturgy showing forth praise-tinted
compassion. . . . .
Yellow lipstick fingers pry into shopkeepers' shutters,
conscious
of mortality.

Valley Deep

Holiness in a night——
rich, furrowed field nursing the dead
winter oak,
dubbing the needle-stubbed pines with false
stealth;
Sadness in a night——
fugitive raindrops pit-pat plaintively,
their dampness seeping into sorrow-weary
thoughts
of my own. . . . .
Peacefulness in a night——
not true peace, for that comes only with
the
light of truth, but cessation.
Nuzzling up to chilled grass, allowing the
cricket
his song, releasing the blades from tread.

And there is justice in the night,
for he leaves no shadows.

Hiding

Where are you hiding? The garden is empty, foliage frothing in lonely desperation, dying; Faces bruised by steel rods of idolatry, of hallowed dependencies that are not holy. . . . . Skulls dented by the wrath of temporality, meshing in nerves of angry pain; The greenery is crying out, O Lord——Where have I been hiding?

Fall 1986

Following

Death as reality——
no longer a fallow field in the distance,
untilled and unheeded;
Suffering as holes in the hand——
the red soil of flesh swallowing air,
showing splintered bones for burnt offerings. . . . .
Obedience as courage——
the blind hurtle into a universe
you have never made acquaintance with but must
trust the design of. . . . .
These are our daily tasks,
for the cross is something
you get nailed to.

Symphony Conductor

Violin foils perch
for battle, the comitatus bowing
to a Cyning of immeasurable grace,
each love-won stroke stirring
the pot of musical mead with pondered clarity,
beauty gleaned from clashing harmony like wheat
pickled from the chaff. . . . .
Elegies tickle the strings,
mourning deep in each thane
as he listens to the lyre of some ancient poet
now resurrected in song;
How long will you crouch in the lairs of your own fear
for your Lord?
And how long will your soul's score abide
in this music hall if you are not
your own master?

Death of a Good Friend

Pluton of scarred rock jutting from the weeping coast——
stony diffraction, the water never quite consumes you;
So also is the mind-monger
who crucified the intellect of the brilliant One,
a good friend of mine.
Crag of disease, it seems the sweltering emotions
rasping at your feet do not sway you——
but I know they are wearing you down:
My friend never wore down.
The discharge of the sea drips from your twisted crevasse,
and for justice's sake, you wear your shame——
My friend was innocent. You killed Him.
Someday, you stupid sick stone,
my friend will salt His bread with the silt
of your destruction.

The Making of the Manger

i

Courtyards bustled,
merchants scurried,
torches were hurriedly lit, breads baked ferociously
in steaming ovens, trinkets were assembled meticulously
on borrowed tables. . . . . the seasonal rush;
This was the season of enrollment——
hordes of grappling, grousing citizens
would stretch the seams of Bethlehem
to be counted, doing their chores and gobbling up the wares
of the teeming city——after all this only happens
once a year;
Somewhere along the way,
in the frenzied rush,
Bethlehem forgot to hear the cries
from a stable,
and thank God for the Baby in manger rags. . . . .
Which season do you celebrate?
Christmas cards and egg nog
or
Jesus in a forgotten manger of your heart
?

ii

Dress-up dolls in neglected bassinets——
objects of affection, never knowing love;
Pine pantheons
awaiting adornment——
We've thrust our heresy upon them,
laden boughs of icy glisten,
heavy,
vulnerable to snapping off.
So the season has begun,
and with pitiful pictures will we partake
of the secret——
The Gift is coming.

iii

The bones of the dwelling spiral gradually,
forming a great vaulting apex——
a cranium of animal stench;
The spine is wooden,
chinked in a few places where animals have whittled away,
bearing the mark of its guests.
The gales gored its tiny frame,
but it wheezed and groaned and stood. . . . .
The crudity, the utter humanity,
was never forgotten, and this made it worth remembering
as the Holy One prepared His entrance
Such a boorish vessel hewn of humble materials——
such a blessed birthplace.

iv

The buttress of the shanty
enveloped its occupants protectively,
containing the sprigs of warmth, battling against
elements and foe——
The Cornerstone with healing in His wings
waits there chanting His Father's words——
I love you, don't forget,
I love you.
Embracing us, the shield of His arm invincible,
gored by relentless heel,
razed with whip,
guarding me.
And as He receives us into His Body,
we are made complete.
Whole.
Royalty.
And so the baby King prepares His servants,
struggling against elements and foe,

Saying,

I love you,
don't forget;
God has spoken.

v

Fashion in us
the heart of Mary,
frightened and trusting,
willing to travel a Way she did not understand
and suffer the degradation of living what she believed. . . . .
And the strength of Joseph——
silent, powerful, faithful;
When there was no room in the inn,
his steps did not falter as he sought the stable
to house the Son of a Father who believed in him,
a simple carpenter, to usher in the kingdom of God.
We grow tired of seeking a cradle to rest our heads,
and Christ is left to His own ends——
Where are you
when the night is cold,
and darkness is laughing,
and your sister is laboring,
and there is no room at the inn?
Where are you when Jesus' life depends on you?

vi

All the day long we waited——
eons of despair gnawed at the tender flesh of hope,
and the maw of evil clawed at us, saying
Come believe in darkness, believe you are the kings of your
universe, believe you will never die——
Still we are waiting for the true King.

Somewhere deep inside our muddled hearts,
we knew the hurt was real, and that Truth, when sought,
will heal.
So we brought the lumber of our spirits,
splintered and diseased, to build a makeshift palace
in order that Truth might have a place to be born;
We brought our hopes and fears,
and laid them at His feet——our only treasure.
We waited for You then, and we wait for You now. . . . .
Our need for healing will never end.
I bring my broken lumber, my forlorn hope, my consuming fear——
These are met in Thee
tonight
and forever.

vii

Silent star
wreathed in your scarlet-burnt blanket,
whetting the slippery edge of Hope
of Faith in things we cannot see;
You shine bright tonight,
your beams burrowing into the mantle of
darkness, to light the way. . . . .
Some did not believe your starlit message was any different
From what we saw on all the other nights, and still they walk in
obscurity——
Some did not bow to the Great Light,
and their nighttime will last forever.
Burn with courage, skystar,
and lead still more children
to the promise
of eternal light.

viii

Prophets spun their tales,
wise men gathered stars for their palatial collections,
and the son of a shepherd held on tightly to the
tatters of his father's cloak——
With rosy cheeks, a naughty smile on his little flushed face,
glowing in the mystery of it all, he snatched
a glimpse of this Baby the angels had raved on about. . . . .
There it was, in the face of a shivering boy,
a most unexpected place for the spirit of
JOY.
Everyone else was in awe, or exuded respect——But this boy
brought to the manger joy
!!!!!!!
Unto us a Child is born!
Hallelujah and Praise!!!
Look, thought the amazed child,
Look at His tiny fingers, and His little face all scrunched up
in wrinkles!
Listen to His irritated gurglings, cooing and cawing
and simply making noise.
I must get back to the sheep before Daddy finds out. . . . .
Oh, Daddy knows all right——
someone had to add to gold,
frankincense and myrrh
the excitement of knowing the wait is over
and the Gift has come.

ix

Bruised, discolored hand
because it touched the raw places.

Strong, spindly veins ruptured,
spilling, soaking into the skin-blanket;
These hands, grown of infant flesh,
immature and unaware
of the fitting for nails.
These hands,
cupped to catch my tears, warm and tender as
they weld
to mine——the securing anchor in my flail of
doubt and darkness. . . . .
These hands,
generation of carpenters,
builder of stables, sawyer of souls.

x

For every garment rolled in blood,
for every separation among men,
for every frustration in weary hearts,
for every blow in angry despair,
He is come.
For the meek,
and the poor,
and the sick,
and the grieving,
and for all sinners,
He is hope.
Mankind will not die any longer the death he has earned
and should rightfully receive,
for He is mercy.
He who knew no sin was made sin,
and His coming, rebirth, is a joy that speaks to us
in the harrowed pits of our human
being. . . . .
We are the words,
believers, for all the lost to
hear——
Sing a new Song this Christmastide,
for He is God,
and He is coming back.

xi

Now with the season ended,
life resumes its disorder, and the sting of shortcoming
is not so sharp. . . . .
But Jesus does not live for us to return to the old iniquity——
We can make Santa Claus the god
of December fun,
and drown in our toys;
Or we can worship Christ,
Redeemer of men,
and rejoice in the knowing that Christmas
has just begun.

Learning to Die

Don't You get tired of teaching me how to die, how to grieve with patience for the unresolved, how to tumble from the treetop. . . . . Hard is the ground, the discipline of dirt in eyelashes, the throbbing temple filled with cancer; I am so sorry for the extra yoke I laid on Your shoulder, but You have not slowed Your step or surrendered the hope that will lead me home. Learning to die is my carving knife that gives life to my canvas———You are my model.

Anger

Winter 1986

Incarnate

We await the carnal flesh to drape You,
folding alabaster bones with pink weaves of form. . . . .
We sit with our symbols in the wilderness, hoping.
Our hearts are expansive, ambiguous
like the lunar mosaic serrated with precipices——
the clouds steepening and recessing to paint the moon
in ascension, tearing their tissue paper advances
like nails drilled through a palm;
Fear becomes the vein that runs away from holiness,
returning without risk to the self-center——
never pumping fresh blood to the fringes. . . . .
I have nothing but my flesh to offer You,
nothing but this wilderness to welcome You. . . . .
You are what we ran away from——
the essence of Emmanuel.

Mother, Father

We are graven on the palms of His hands,
the bitter gully of a nail's relentlessness;
Our lives have been hammered into His one life,
and a Mother's sucking child
will not be forgotten by the womb. . . . .
She Herself suffers bitterly,
but we will not be denied our milk.
No longer does the canyon of death
keep us from Her side,
and He walks among the galaxies
with our humanity
engraved in His hands.

The Misunderstood Sisters

G: Sometimes I am threatened by your gifts,
the beauty you lend to me. . . . .
Promise alive with love
rests in your long hand, the bone-perfect fingers
at ease with the potential;
How I love you——
how I bask my wilting youth in your new morning,
how I am loved.

J: Your brokenness is the poultice for your wincing wounds,
though you know it not.
The depths you abide in have enriched my height,
the weeping of your heart mingling
with the quiet of my pity and compassion
to make us whole——
Sometimes I am afraid you will shy away from me,
and no longer will I know the wrenching purity
of your emotion, and I will forget
the warmth of light because I cannot taste darkness
in my tears for you. . . . .
How you strengthen me——
how I am thankful for your hard-won lessons,
how you are strong.

Grief never journeys without her soulmate Joy,
and neither holds Promise in her hand
without wanting to give it to the other——

they love, though that threatens the spectrum that separates
their identity——they know they are not complete
unless they are One.

Count Down

A thousand tears have come and gone,
and I am not yet empty.
The tide of foaming pain-laced sorrow
has pommeled the sand of my refuge,
yet I am not beaten.
The salt of despair has soured upon my tongue,
though I am not spoiled.
The flowers of my soul-field have known the raging
tempest,
and are not broken;
The old year has passed,
and the contract is renewed. . . . .
Time,
though you are the length of my suffering,
you are not the depth,
and in the new age,
I will be crowned
with the glory of my enduring grief.

Shuttle 1986

Sky curtain
in the temple of man's thirst for knowledge
cudgeled
with the bloated, swelling heat
of a flaming horror——
Trembling, wobbling, incinerating,
poof.
All gone——
eye of discovery torn from the socket of
frontier space,
vanished,
snowing terrible ashes from the clash
with the unknown, the unknowable,
death;
The life of this quest,
loosed from the sooty bonds of earth to
touch the face of God,
rest now at His left hand.
Not so long ago
was another curtain rent, exploding
across the centuries a message of hope. . . . .
Lives in this journey,
we will continue the search for the face
you now behold——
Burial sky,
keep us not from hoping.

Acceptance

There was an owl in the church
when I went to pray. . . . .
Pensive, wide-eyed, without sound;
I prayed about promises,
and wanting to feel protected about
the ME they were threatening to take away;
I prayed about wills,
and frustrating grief,
and tension.
I remembered
His care, joy, peace and His last
words——
Unto Thy hands I commit My spirit.
The watchful owl
and I
whispered
Thy Will Be Done.

Amen.

Our New Union

No longer forsaken or desolate, wedded to the nature of beauty and truth and wisdom and the Supreme Love, I bask in my blessed inheritance; Lord Jesus, You have taught me that my former heritage is only a dying stem in the wind, and our new union calls me chosen, priest, endowed. Help me wear this humble badge with the mind of Christ, sincere love for the brothers and integrity of relation, giving of myself even as You first gave to me.

Bound to the Vine

Tiny branches on the beautiful, mysterious Vine——bound inescapably to You unless we cut ourselves off. . . . . Sometimes my fear threatens to whittle my life down until my fibers are thin, and I snap off. But You have held on to me even in the strongest wind, and not this storm nor any other shall burn the root of my fruit, for You died to make it so——make me resilient, Lord, and when the Vine reaches heaven, accept this, my humble branch.

I Call You Master

Father, glorify Thy name and not my own. . . . . So many times I have nailed my name to the cross to claim the power when Your body is still upon it—— So many nails we are still driving in You; You made me Your friend, not Your substitute, and though You live through me, I am not fit to untie the thong of Your sandal, O Lord——not then, and not now. The suffering I endure, I endure because of You, not in place of You: Teach me, Christ Jesus, the truth——even as You call me friend, I call You Master.

The Silent Prophetess

Portents pondered in a virgin's heart, unrealized miracles waltzing in the atrium, thumping with insipid shoes on parquet floors waxed with spirit. . . . . Magnificent Magi, glittering and humble though not yet wise enough to clothe their strength in weakness——but wise enough to know where to learn; Mary was the silent prophetess who knew the world would not learn to dance until the Bridegroom widowed His bride and the Son gave back His feet to the Father.

Spring 1987

The Leap

Steel unbelief the color of lean pine bark
pinioned the feathers, and made her forget
the color of the sky.
Orange emeralds lay blunted in the white foam
of her wings as she scudded
from the radiance of the wind——
faith cannot fly its true colors
if it hides from the gale. . . . .
In the crunching moment
when steel was pried from stone
the dove emerged, tiny, tense,
afraid of beauty and faithful——
Suffer the wind
or surrender the universe.

Trading Torches

A fourth man in the furnace
and silver-maroon flames twining tongues
to squeeze us.
We've aligned ourselves with death,
brutalized by the fight
and borrowing dignity to resist
at least the flame of hate. . . . .
We face our russet equinox
wanting to believe that while the skin
gushes
from our bones in an exodus of pink sadness,
the hierarchy of the universe will shift to equal
length,
and what is ruined will be regal;

There is an extra victim, though,
a companion that glows
with internal fire,
a gift from God.
He is telling us with words distorted
by heat that pierces His side seeking water
that we can be whole through the fire,
mortal yet meaningful,
forgiving without forsaking.
The keeper of the well revived us
and the door opened to the king——
Untouched, absolved of the stench of consumption,
we marveled at the man
who remained to defy flame,
to die in our furnace.

Penance

Bamboo ladders and Teflon hillsides
repel a foothold with muddy indignation
at your courage. . . . .
Your sins hang from your shoulder,
and their scourge is the slipperiest
of all rockfaces;
You are facing
with grief akin to the purple rage of morning
the ones with the key to forgiveness,
and you are waiting
for them to kill you.
Your body is already broken
by the weight you gave it,
and the poverty of your spirit is the slum
you wanted to deserve——
The knife is slashing, and the ones you sinned against
have set you free.

Disease

Ruined beauty haggling
for a few tokens of appreciation,
skin divided by man-made pipes while breasts
heave in the horror of breathing. . . . .
Robes hemmed in scarlet make a scarecrow
from ganglion legs and witlessly defeated
head teetering on a shoulder bone——
the birds don't even bother.
Thoughts like gas
prowl into recesses, taunting
any fairytale hope of scarecrows climbing
down from their sticks and seeing the sun.
When there are memories there are crows
to give the field at least existence,
something to shoo.
You hung me here with a knife
and a piece of my heart——
I never had the chance
to be beautiful.

Void

Thorny aberration,
you are black like invisible rain at
midnight,
opaque and infinite in a pyramid
of non-definition. . . . .
I hear you wheeze when my foot tipples at the turret
looking for the love that made me——
I toss you fish like a peacemaker
with seals.
I will never forget the gulp
that meant the end of my dream
and the start of your meaning. . . . .
I will not come back here and feed
you pieces of my identity, or ask you
what love was when you formed me——
there are some places
we cannot go.

Tomorrow's Farewell

Waving to trains
on their fossilized vinyl tracks,
each tie soaking the heat of their black escape,
the air simmering as the steaming
metal
shoots through like blown glass;
A fugitive from bitterness,
running in the heat of the spirit,
unwilling to pull in the pistons because
tomorrow might come too
soon. . . .
You cannot flee forever, rebellious house,
and on the other side of gall
is the coolness of peace, beckoning.
Wave only with your hand——
the whistle is blowing,
and the station closes soon.

Letting Go

Unbind me
          from these stripes of suffering,
     this gauze of bitterness. . . . .
Like cat paws that crease the straw,
          my hope is tentative, flinching
               at the noise. . . . .
If only You had come
     before my eulogy was begun,
          the horse clad in thunder
     might not have sought a fresh rider;
If only You had healed me the first time,
          my body would not have blended
               with the disease. . . . .
Our ways are not Your ways,
          and the new creature who emerged
     from bandaged bindings
  strides in firm hope
               across the straw.

All Day Friday

Cobbler of innocence,
pasting fallen with free,
one of three;
You broke the chain of shame,
and touched with Your ungnarled fingers
the fist of guilt and failure, declawing its thrust. . . . .
Your name is Jesus,
and all day Friday You descended into hell
that the tender eyes of Your sheep might gaze
once again on the glory of Him who sent You,
He who sends us. . . . .

We are bound in that innocence,
anointed with trust,
baptized with Friday's blood. . . . .
That pure, prefallen twinkle
lodged in the lapis edge of Your eye
seals our brotherhood, Friend, wedding us in the memory
of broken hands.

The Mortality of Lightning

Incandescent biers of friction
explode in silence through the night air——
how lonely the lightning is without thunder. . . . .
Like the brother
who faces the death-bolt
without the sound of his sibling's voice——
Why can't we share our sonship. . . . .
We die together, children of light,
and with our hands nestled as one
in a numinous nap, we shall assemble with the Savior——
I will be waiting for you
in whatever tomorrow you awake to,
and we will embrace in light
that is no longer fleeting.

Picking a Plot

Yellow cotton and carrion
grown together in the mesa
like a caesura among cycles——
the inhaled breath pairing
oxygen with waste places. . . . .
Each topaz flower is a word, hope
held in brain-cell stasis,
pent expression;
Each carcass fumes and gropes,
their visions screaming from the filmy bones,
the death that instructs life.
Come with me when I return
to this terraced sward,
and let's share two voices
with one truth——
words and wildflowers
are all I have left.

Three Hours of Estrangement: The Travail of Twelve

Valedictions creasing cloth
on sunburned shoulders, weary feet, awaiting
breakfast. . . . .
Movements of the moon's love
pare the solar system's center——
God squeezes light out of one
moment,
and they fall in fetus fashion to be humbled. . . . .
Sarcophagous hope blisters
fishermen hands, tormenting
visions of armies and thrones
when only a wooden pole would do for a
kingdom seat;
They brought their goodbyes to you
only to find them deathless,
their limitations of what God can do
eclipsed.

Hiding Place

Tussocks cloister about the mouth
of a shriven creek bed, exposed roots draped
only
in a negligee of crumb dust. . . . .
Plows don't burrow here anymore,
the Ant-dynasty holding hard reign of this
sanctuary;
Flows don't run here any longer,
for they are weary, grown faint.
With a futile body I draw near to this place,
designing my own grassy crown,
allowing the ant his evil——
You have come to meet me,
bearing all the shades of Sheol in Your body,
and I mount up with the wings of eagles,
exposed and unending.

The Leaping Lame

Ballerinas of light leap
in the frozen expression of an
asymptote,
a frilly statue to the lame who have no
dance. . . . .
Thin arms pluck at stars and make no sound,
their graceful sweeps beckoning the inner
voice
to raise its own liturgy;
Legs darkened by silence
lie restlessly in the dust,
waste places now in the motion of life.
From a wheelchair I watch the sun
cast a plié in the glass,
turning my scars into stars
and assuring me of a day
for the leaping lame.

To You and Back Again

i

The tip of a murky taper flagellates with kinetic purpose,
urgently dragging even weak light to the corpse of darkness. . . . .
he wonders who keeps that candle,
and why they should seek his cave to store
flasks of tenderness;
Platonic shadows pretend to be more than illusions,
dying as the flame wriggles——but not rising again.
Spiderwebs do not grow here, the gossamer shackling wandering hands
and spiders recanting their pocket-homes for they know the loneliness
of this cave. . . . .
he listens for every unsure step, but makes no sound,
praying wordlessly he will and will not
be found.

ii

Suddenly there she is,
a doe nursing her taper, an angel awaiting wings.
She's fought the images to believe the truth,
and he's here——beyond the shadows.
She hasn't come to abide,
but to offer her light of knowledge, her love of all life.
Her fingers flinch as wax singes them,
realizing aloneness may very well be her wholeness——
She leaves the candle beside him
and holds the invisible hand that lifts her to the ledge
where she can finally hear his voice. . . . .

To her he quietly sings——
an angel is adorned
with wings.

Inclement Weather

You were playing in the snow,
the rich malty powder a perfect mortar
for your sandbox fortress. . . . .
I watched you toss your newfound manna
into the bright air, content and enthralled to trace
angels in the nourishing flakes;
It was not even winter, but season could not deprive you
of the joy of inclement weather——
Heavy skies reeled around you, but the sun was your rainy-day playmate,
and he showered delight upon you even in your chamber of darkness. . . . .
You are the child in me
that plays in the place where youth perished
and where the hurt makes snow fall

in summer.

The Still Small Voice

There was a wind that brought me to my knees, tickling the bullet holes that broke me. . . . . There was a shaking of all substance, toppling every stone of importance and crushing every vestige of peace; There was a fire that grabbled at hope, scratching and scorching the tender membranes of the throat that would call to You. And then there was a sound that seemed to me a hiss, a slow exhalation of promise that squeaked in its simplicity and roared in the vitality of truth———the still small voice.

In the Land of Silence

In the land of silence there dwells a gallant beggar, a shadow among the smug, a relentless peacemaker among the bitter. . . . . The ones who think they speak are the ones he collects coins for, peddling with his leaky crown a purchase of peace. He will come to your house and entreat you to live without ever speaking, hunched and smiling because he is dancing to music you must know death to hear.

Psalm 42

With a deadly wound in my body, I make a prayer to the God of my life. . . . . Why go I mourning? Why hast Thou forgotten me? A multitude is keeping festival, taunting me for the scars of my naked wound, spitting sarcastically 'Where is your God?' Indeed, I wonder and I hurt in my aloneness, but I will defend my love for You until the close of the age, for I know You are just, and true, and You are always with me. My soul is cast down and disquieted within me——I shall again praise Him.

Lift Up My Head, Lord

Broken in spirit, gasping in cruel bondage, I seek Yahweh—— my mangled head hangs in pain on my breast, life quivering in the chest cavity, pushing out but afraid of the death beyond its boundaries. . . . . The cancer is growing, incising nerves, a scythe on my stem, harvesting no good fruit; Lift up my head, Lord, distorted and weary, that I might press wine into Pharaoh's hand——Keep cancer from hanging me.

Psalm 22

Wax hearts and cleaving tongues possess Your people, Lord, and they refuse to hear Your name amid affliction. . . . . I am laid low in the dust of death, yet I will praise You in the congregation——You art enthroned in those feeble attempts at glorification, and Your patience unto perfection is infinite; Eli, Eli, You have not forgotten. Save us not from death, but from dying without our Lord.

You Are My Lord

You are my courage and my compassion. My God and my life, Your sides are indeed deep, and Your tendons are tense from the nail-razing. . . . .You are my strength and my salvation. You live that I might not die, and no mist will hide Your guiding hand; Bolster me to a life of passionate humility, a creature before a beast, a new creation.

I Intend to Smile in Sickness

I tire of sorrow, the rupture of dawn by self-satisfaction——
oozing purple where saffron should reign. . . . . I weary of
sackcloth, and ashes that dirty my eyelids——blink, blink, water,
water. Ennui destroys more youth than does disease——I intend
to smile in sickness and rescue the dawn from ennui.

Summer 1987

Narcissus

Mustard daffodils with mayonnaise edges
hang on to the convulsing air with
their teacups-for-faces,
and don't mind the bending. . . . .
They have no tragic amulet to wear
like roses have thorns,
nor can they pour a potion of gleaming cream
on a well-wisher's finger like torn cactus;
The lesson they have learned
since that day at the river
is the sorrow that feeds their top-heavy quiver——
living symbols of the tyranny
self-devotion can become. . . . .
It is no wonder you cannot lift your face
to the sun.

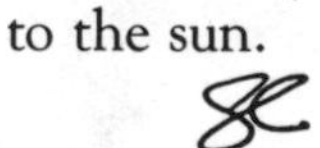

A Woman's Crucifixion

Afraid of ugliness,
tense at the thought of tenderness
or tryst that would test
womanhood.

I swam with you in the
waters beneath my brain and waited
to feel the splash of subtle
rejection. . . . .

The murky drip of desire
slimes into a heart of hopelessness,
a court-jester announcing
dawn.

We create the space of
encounter, the holiness of supping with
another's cup——ambivalence
breaking.

A kiss means betrayal
if laughter is obsolete and you
refuse relations with
grief;

My ugliness will not drown you,
though you must perceive beauty beneath the bolts
the world has used to tie me

on a tree

atop a hill,

left to die.

Poetic Prison

Silence might have been our bondsman
    if I had let you tell me
    you loved me without using words. . . . .

Instead the sun came up and there was
    conversation, deep and blue with yellow
    smiles, tittering and teasing.

We wrestled with angels but you refused
    to bless me——the seething white edges
    of the cloud we were to wed screamed

At the hole we left in the sky
    as we fell to destruction
    in a kiss created with words
        and a communion

    that could not bind

    yellow and blue

        into green.

Abide

Golden cutlery buttering summer leaves
in the place where myths live,
a hallowed pocket of meaning
in an expanse of separation——
sun setting.
Nearing You
in the green snow is the hark and call
of my hope as it is here
I've come to watch and pray. . . . .
Omniscience, You come to us in creation
with salvation bleeding in Your hands
and 'abide' upon Your lips——
heart against heart
and love ex nihilo.
Sun slicing summer trees
while I watch to be near You
on bleeding knees.

SC

The Circle Sister Drew

Beauty:

You are waiting
for the moon to disappear and
the sun
to take its place beside hope.
But you shine with the very heat
of your barrenness,
aglow with the burden that
sears your mask——
a form I pour substance
into. . . . .
You are not haunted
by sunshine though your reflection is
the only light
that makes me real. . . . .
My surface is unknown
without your depth, and I would
never know the new
without the haggard lines
of your ageless waiting——
to behold you is to weep for the moon,
the dust of eternal night.

Ugliness:

I hailed you in the height of fear
and heard the stone you dropped
on my reflection. . . . .
You are the dew that comes before sundown,
glistening and radiant on the freshly
sown fields;
I watch you
when you sing on the
mountain——
I cannot be jealous of a song
that thirsts for wisdom or a heart
that showers the earth with
righteousness. . . . .

I am the night nourished by your dew,
the morning glory risen
from brier brambles.
I would never seek the light
without your beacon,
the mercy of the stone you threw
that drew strength
from a life of weakness.

Hugging the Harrow

Close to death from my youth up,
my hands are upon the plow
and I've never looked back;
The furrows I till resemble
the dying mounds that braid my skull——
quite a different field to farm. . . . .
You have bound me with the
pinions and plumage of love,
corpulent and encompassing,
my wings for flying alone;
I'm used to dying——
bedside, graveside.
It was when I saw the sorrow
glisten in Your eye
that I knew I could fly——
unalone.

Evening Litany

The Son of man seeks rest
from the multitude,
the beloved of God who want not
His love;
The refugee strokes
her blameless child, gaunt and guilty only
of the right to live. . . . .
The cancer victim
seeks the sunset,
the holy indigo of peace,
the sad amber stilling the mockery
of life entrenched in death;
I am that victim,
and I see Your footsteps in the firmament——
sunset nettles are the soft bedding
where the Son of man
lays His head.

Dance

Your face is gruff against mine,
matted beard relaying living drops
to my smooth cheek,
a comforting forest to drink from
in the raped wasteland. . . . .
The muscles in Your jaw
are firm and tired from wincing——
the hours You spent moving Your mouth
in unutterable lamentation;
Your feet question not their destination
nor doubt the grace of wisdom
that informs Your step,
yet You chose to falter
when my body could not go on. . . . .
Your long day at the river,
wringing the cloths with which we cover
ourselves
quenching the burning facade of fallenness
with liquid voice
feet twisting in sand shifting,
muddied waters——
The love You sprinkled on them then
is the music pressed between our faces,
my baptism into the holy allemande You began
two thousand years ago.

Longing for Sleep

I remember the ice darkness unable to cool my heat-frenzied head;
My life aspirations were reduced to the longing for sleep, the sweet
reprieve of unconsciousness. . . . . Family came and went——
their love did penetrate my pain, but I could not succumb to their
shocked grief——not yet. Jesus never left my little bedtable, and
He would stroke my face when it was hot, and shut out the
sounds when they hurt my healing. Now I know Him and
praise Him in the land of the living, but my body won't let
my spirit forget to grieve reluctantly for darkness.

Peace

Fall 1987

Bridegroom

Your cheek is feverish and damp, my lips
bruising tenderness with their need to
remember——
I so want to love You,
denials ringing, betrayal stinging
and thirty silver pieces singing the aria
of my unworthiness;
Your back curdles under gouged-out stripes,
scabs rising to rip for the
snake-sharpness of the whip——
I'm pressing with my arms
to ease the flow,
but embraces do not save the dying.
Here I am. Presence. Anniversary.
Sorry.

River Crossing

Tomorrow may not come,
the moorings of soul to body
slipping weakly into the moss-covered water. . . . .
Death will not be a rending,
a violent thrashing among the iron reeds,
a bloody regurgitation of what I hoped life would be;
Nor will I die a tranquil death——
disease has seen to that.
I shall remove my shoes, undress my breath,
shut off my veins and toss my hat. . . . .
At His feet I timidly offer
the life He esteemed so greatly——
there will be no sting.
The morrow may demand
my humanity, my earthly identity:
I will not die drowning.

I Heard Him Walking

Dark pilgrims in the glory patch,
hearing a foot pad softly upon foliage,
making a way through the garden. . . . .
I cannot face Him,
confessions pounding against my inadequacies,
unworthy to hear His tread;

I must not run from Him,
the small bud of courage knowing
it can survive only in this soil.
There is a voice lowing——
Respond to Me,
be alive.

He is walking in your garden,
stitching garments to soothe your shame,
hurting in the aloneness of His
image. . . . .
When you curl up at His feet, respond
and remember He is alive.

Child of the Covenant

I laid you at His feet heavily,
feeling the hole somewhere inside
unstitch itself and gape open. . . . .
I kissed your forehead and held
the crippled hand always silent in life
but strangely expressive in death;

It was but a whisper that evaporated through that hole——
God bless you and keep you
and make His face to shine upon you
and give you peace. . . . .
Long before I made this journey, you gave yourself
to Him as a gem to gird His crown——He did
not steal you.
I turned around once, flesh of my flesh taken so young,
to cry one last tear for the cancerous
hole——
God will keep us
and give us peace.

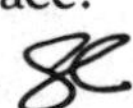

Lazarus Returned

Skin dripping from your face,
hands quivering at your sides,
bandages tousled and disarrayed. . . . .
O my beaten soldier-man——
the battle you fought transcended time, spanning terrain untouched
by finitude——
I heard you singing to passerby suns,
and I could not help saying a final goodbye;
I've missed you, brave friend,
but I know you must return to truth,
the mead of hope soothing your lips,
filling your hunger. . . . .
I will remember,
and I will wait.
You were my other half,
disease freeing you and leaving me
to fight a different front;
We have life in each other's memory, but very soon we will be joined
in the perfect union——
Me,
my greater self,
and our Shepherd.

Hope Has Begun

There in the vast grazing range,
bracing for the cold of iniquity,
huddled in the mist-kissed grass,
trying to keep track of my scattered sheep,
alone.
There in the infinite pasture of living,
clutching to the whims of breezes,
buried in the furrowed soil,
cascading from cloud-beds,
A Promise clung to the sham of
Earth-life.
I and It,
Me and He,
Us and the three of
Them. . . . .
Sharing the bitter tear
and swell of fear——
Angels spoke of the Creator's promise
to bear the burden,
and warm my shame,
and gather the sheep
There
in Shepherd's Field.

Save Us From Our Self-Reliance

We get so accustomed to our human limits, Lord, sometimes we try to limit You. Sometimes we impose our befuddled notion of what life should be on the Great Design of what life will someday become, and we scribble over it like four-year-olds in fingerpaint; But still You are patient, and loving, and forgiving. Thank You. Save us from our self-reliant abominations——bring the kingdom in even through us, Your ignoble vessels.

The Final Feast

A long table lifts its cup to You, my Lord, in remembrance; Many are seated at Your banquet——different skins and different sights, all placing their fingertips upon Corpus Christi, *repenting. . . . . An expectant and excited people await the final feast,* God of my life, *and we crown You King——our lives replace the thorns You once wore. . . . . Broken for You.*

I Will Not Despair

On the skirts of the earth Your light unto the nations waxes and wilts not in discouragement; Our hearts are weak, Lord, as we try to tell You where to lay the ocean's bounds, to hew the cornerstone, to shed a tear. . . . You had no lessons to learn, for all truth lines Your garment, and justice is Your rod. Be patient with me, even me, as I ponder on this devastating lesson——though I am not kept from death, by Your might I will not despair.

Death Unsung

Stones of torment
splintering the frieze of safety,
the health of a betrayed body,
the security of time. . . . .
Heavy stones,
like tumors sunk in the mire
of turncoat cells,
splattering without remorse love-won pieces;
I cannot promise you I will not die——
do not kill me before I am through with
life. . . . .
Failure purloins peace,
but I do not have to die
for your entropy——
I am tired
of picking up pieces.

The Divorce of Mercury

The ideology of planets glares
from the corners of creation,
its great cosmic berth accommodating
the sum of all parts. . . . .
It is vision,
it is mystery
and it is infinite fascination
with the bitterness of fragments
and the delicacy of a whole;
I drink its assertions
with astronaut wonder,
chilled to my inmost core upon feeling the colors
of our cobalt sphere——
I am the hoping one.
Stellar hearts dance
in their orbits, lovers of space but frustrated
with one-way rotation. . . . .
Solar fear endangers
the instruments of healing, for planets don't want
to be vulnerable in the face of searing barbs
and burnt-out trust.
I will tolerate the mystery,
rejoice within my orbit
and dare to bask in the sun——
don't abandon
the hoping one.

Desertion

I wish I had known you
when your quiver of truth drew dry——
arrows denied a destination,
thrust into the marrow of what you thought you wanted. . . . .
Character had been the mettle
that kept your world from caving in,
but when the first stone fell
and sliced the stagnant waters in your forgotten cavern
you laid down your armor and
strangled the crossbow that brought you here. . . . .
I wish I could have told you tomorrow would still come,
stones will still be thrown
and the enemy will not lay down arms
in the wake of your surrender;
I wish I could have offered you
the face you shattered when
the cavern crumpled and I
had to watch the hope that conceived me
sputter and die.
You never wanted to know
what I had to give you,
or who it was
that threw the first stone.

Peter's Widow

Gluttons for motion lap without lips
against a heart made for floating,
a dock that rests amid the shaking.
A woman carved by salt
wrings the bedclothes with vigor,
knuckles whitening, fingers sticky
with seawater stains. . . . .
She knows the tide rises,
consuming souls in a human storm
and mastering whatever tenderness is left
until bereft of holiness.
She cannot help her twisting,
fisting furor with her washbasket——
snow does not fall on sand,
and someone must do the cleaning. . . . .
Lot's wife lifts her hand
to salute twilight's breeze,
letting her intensity suffice
until he comes again.

Brain Surgery

Pink and squealing, tissue
bubbles up to the incision——the strata of
every aspiration separating in the coarse light
and dangling in the peril of exposure. . . . .
It took an earthquake to crack the skull
that afternoon, sawing into glory
and gnawing at the integrity
of the universe;
The cortex tore so easily, undressing
the holiest of sanctuaries by shearing
the curtain of thought in two——
scooping the jelly of all that really mattered,
a drawn and quartered collection of the image
first fashioned by the head
that sags open and bleeding on a wooden
table. . . . .
When that first cell fell
to the scalpel of our self-delusion,
midnight aborted noon
and the heavy sighs of a Father grieving
bristled across the auditorium
of silence;
Orbits and sockets squeezed into swollen purple caskets,
battlescars of war between worlds
and turrets on a castle assaulted
by the squeamish vinedressing of dawn——
did Your eyes seal You up too?
We were both imprisoned
in the gritty tombs of gossamer,
message leaping to messenger in hollow
reverberation——where did they put us?
Clanking echoes of the web You untangled
still pad about in the tunnels of my brain,
and I find solace for their emptiness
in the creature You left behind and
suffered birth for;

She was quite tiny, You know,
until this new space unmeshed itself
and she was allowed
to grow.
Did they stitch You back together
with promises too, refusing to travel
with You back to the tomb
to remember——I see You
every time I sit in my tunnel, the Head
we violated
on Calvary.

Martha

Heat and hurry rippling
over her face, the earnestness
of her serving carving the identity she
will wear;
She gives it all at once,
her love,
her enthusiasm,
her weariness.
She cannot ignore the needs of the body,
rushing to fulfill her spirit by easing hunger——
the homeless are not just her capitalistic
excuses.
She is unused to drinking
from the chalice slowly, and instead of pondering
she wonders why peace does not mean
rest from toil. . . . .
She flees the tension
of grace and graciousness,
unwilling to abide in the paradox
of tenderly tough love;
She has served Him well, and given Him everything
except vulnerability.

Mary

Sandals, dusty and smitten with toil, are dropped by the door——
The smells of freshly baked bread and new wine float silently through the air;
I am tired and I need peace;
The Man at the table can give it, I know. . . . .
His words are edged with the gentility of the sea and curls of sunlight vein His hands. . . . .
His eyes are sensitive
and He makes the dead places in me alive;
What shall I give in return for His warmth?
She gave Him her own costly ointment for burying her darkness
and she rested at His feet and listened. . . . .
The lesson she learned that day
is that it is as blessed to receive
as to give.

Tears of a Virgin

January is whooshing under seacrop skies,
salmon-roasted and alone with the shame of decay. . . . .
Mother of mothers keeps in a coffer
the death of spring, and a choice for joy;
Centuries have not dimmed her eyes
to the alienating irreverence,
to the crucifixion of children
for guiltless astonishment.
The residue of the universe
is still within her womb, and Thy will be done
will ring in her ears for millenniums to come.
Small tinges of grief
burn through acrylic and oil in a
magnificat of sad fury——
the Madonna weeps for You yet, Yeshua. . . . .
Return
and comfort her.

Five Wounds

Down at the gate Beautiful
the lame man twists, his shredded nerves
absentminded and unable to move the body he has
come to hate. . . . .
No support given him,
no strolling passerby sitting awhile to receive
his tragedy with understanding ears——
there is his agony.
Sons and daughters of the one Father,
this is the downtown doorstop on the way to
the office,
a brisk lunch, the parking lot;
You claim the real and eternal joy
of salvation, the bright news that
He is risen, Hosanna in the Highest.
These promises are yours, my peers,
and they live through you to be given
away. . . .
Christ is come again——
where is your agony
?

Where Are the Angels?

Shrill peal sinking into the fodder and dirty hay
like dust settling on archaic furniture,
crying to the desolation about Him I am alive,
I am real and touchable——infant-omnipotence
not an illusion for Him. . . . .
Darkness, biting breezes, shepherds with sniffles,
grunting cattle, disappointment,
half-heartedness——
these were the murals He was painted into
when He awoke from the womb He was never completely a part of;
These were the first ribbons
strewn across the floor on Christmas morning, hopelessness
the stocking He came to stuff.
He's met the child in each one of us, His own eyes
widening at the wonder of a star——
the star that each child knows burns just for them. . . . .
He knows we garnish trees and stalk the stores——
He's hoping that when we come
to whisper I love You at the cradle,
our eyes will widen too.

What a Name

All in a name, the majesty, the kinghood, Alpha, Omega, the holding together. . . . . We praise Thee, so goes the ancient slogan, We are saved, the ancient story; And in that name we tie up everything we've ever wanted, or needed, or betrayed. And the humdrum characters in the play of Time are for those other people——you know, the lost ones. . . . . Such a Sanhedrin attitude. We praise Thee, Jesus, Christ child, even in our obscene traditions——What a name.

Remove the Scales

Something like scales is falling from my eyes, Lord——the final purge of persecuting evil. . . . . I will gather them in a cup and give them over to a wiser hand, trusting You to take them and free my sight. The road to Damascus hovers in my memory, the lesson of darkness to learn light; Heal, Lord God, the waste places, and remove the scales from our hearts.

Love Conquers All

Weeping is finished with wasting, and I draw near to You full with fear and trembling, flinching at every whisper the tumor utters; You tear down with carpenter's hands the white spiked fence that is my hiding place. . . . . You unbind me unto the world, shaking with vulnerability and bald head——to call them to compassion. With my fear I will go to Your world, Lord, and find that in being afraid with, not of, my brother, I am free. Love conquers all——You are my hiding place.

The Least of Them

I don't know if I'm humble enough to hearken at angel voices in a lonely field where life-and-death care is given to the least of beasts. . . . . Can I cross the transom of the stable if I'm the one who told them there was no room at the inn? Maybe my Lord won't like my gifts, for they were bought as objects when they should've been subjects of my being; I may not be worthy to meet the Messiah at His abode, and that is why He welcomes me—— Our Lord was born and died for the least, for the beast.

Spring 1988 *through* *Fall* 1989

Art Lesson

On the intellectual planet we share
like some Monet, I can compete with you and sail away
from those picturesque images on black river
ice. . . . .
The mental galaxy we live in is not a boat
we can just get in like the capsule boats leaves
resort to when they fall into the river;
But unlike those unused shells of spring-birth,
my physical husk is no longer
buoyant——
if a nut falls on me, I'll surely drown. . . . .
But I can scrap with you on the planet, in the
galaxy,
of the universe where Impressionists
paint.

Jungle Progeny

I couldn't tell you
how you made me feel
or how the raindrops shed abroad
are to this day treasured
in a Styrofoam cup. . . . .
Miracles are so often silent,
slinking into our hurried lives like leopards leaving
the sanctum of animal power
to lie down in a world of men;
You didn't even realize
the comfort your heart placed upon mine——
the Spirit uses even unwanted passion
to make men listen. . . . .
The miracle you gave to me
brought rainbows to my eyes
in the sight
of mother leopard prowling home
to hope.

The Cave

Bats of betrayal hang sullenly
from rafters that connect us to the spiritual,
waiting to flap and flutter at any truth that may want
to cross over——we spend our lives trying
to trap these elusive creatures, though we
turn our backs on the vampires
we created with our dishonesty. . . . .
We try to bridge the gap
between the physical and spiritual, the mental and emotional,
with claps of doctrine and learning until we remember
bats are blind.

Zoo Lessons

An owl emerges from the tangerine shadows,
white and speckled by what he has endured,
boxed in by darkness but seeing what
humanity
has done to itself. . . . .
One wonders what the owl plaid
would say if clad with a voice that didn't cackle
like an old woman at the market;
Would he divulge what he saw in the tabernacle of night?
Would he tell us that he saw
us give our existence away
because we could not face the darkness
that comes before dawn?
We are afraid
because the fluffy owl might spawn
sadness
if we let the speckles
have their say.

The Magi

In the pink desert of an evening sky
indigo camels carry a treasure
too precious to expose to sunlight
and too ordinary to be led by starlight——
after all, what would a King want with my gifts?
As day slips into darkness
we take our fear to the manger,
along with the gold, frankincense and myrrh. . . . .
The sun drowns in the pink desert
and we watch the dragons of our fear,
scaled with shadows and shiny from sunburn,
claw at the camels' flanks and breathe fire
on the manger until we recognize
that these are not just ordinary
barnyard animals.

My Inner Editor

No——I refuse to show you the place
where my storyteller wind blows, where my muse
draws strength from the fountain of Life
and I am kept alive by making despair a metaphor
for release and silence. . . . .
The chrysalis around my personality tore,
so this place of inspiration is not only a
sanctuary
but also a tomb;
I withdraw into my essence, apprehensive like a trapped
sneeze
because I am afraid someone might have followed
me. . . . .
When I return to your level, I must please
and conform to your idea of what a sick person
should be;
No——I will not open the door to my inner
sanctum,
only to have you tease my thoughts and kick dust
in my garden,
as if it were summer and there was more dust where that
came from. . . . .
I am the judge in this place because Jesus can
overrule
me——
Just because you praise me, I don't have to like you,
and it is a daily struggle not to label you as an
intruder——
we don't have seasons here anymore since winter took up
permanent residence.

SC

Apocalypse

When was it that I picked Your veins apart,
squeezing the unction and silent tissue
until You could bleed righteousness no
more. . . . .
Was it really my bitterness
and self-disgust that created vinegar
to pinch Your lips and tempt You to thirst?
Is it possible
I peeled Your dignity with a spear like a potato
because I thought the world had done it
to
me——
I couldn't see the difference kingdom would
make;
Might I have been the soldier
that helped kill You
by standing around in the bliss of status
quo. . . . .
and then believed too late?
But it never is the complete end with You——
Our century has learned
to crucify You with abstracts.

Condemned to Live

The room I live in
has very cold marble floors and a high vaulted ceiling,
with a bay window on the east and the west——
an eye that opens and closes in all seasons. . . . .
The ascetic that is my imagination
squats nakedly on that clammy floor
because she can see the Alpha and Omega of my dreams that way;
How dare you
bounce your ball in here,
or try to tell me what curtains to hang
on my windows——
only I know how to steer when the windows fog
with escapism and no one knows
the pangs of helplessness
that sent me here in the first place;
You told me I had to die, and when I didn't comply,
you sentenced the ascetic of my mind to this little room
and locked me in from the outside——
you thought you could define presence
as a physical reality. . . . .
When you threw your balls at my windows in a rage
I batted them down with a broom——
I hate to tell you, but my spirit can reside and function
even in a tomb.

The Solstice

Half of me, in a kind of plague,
suffers from the extinction of the sun
and clutches helplessly at the
bottles of courage set out at dawn
like the milkman and his daily delivery——
but he won't deliver broken bottles. . . . .
A parasite destroys me,
like the demon justice of the dark side
of creation, cleansing while scrubbing;
That parasite is mutilated pride, the reason darkness comes
so soon
in fall——
the false sense of safety before winter. . . . .
Dawn gives me stimuli to wrestle with like angels and
ladders,
but when the sun is dead, the sap of creation leaks
unchecked from broken bottles.

Snake Burrows

I have to pay an emotional price
every time I board the ferry
and cross over to your world, like sunshine
after a thunderstorm, frustrated
because the humans only recall
the humidity, not the warmth, it brought. . . . .
Rice grains of color litter the shore as I pass,
caught
illuminating our existence when
they should stamp the status quo with approval. . . . .
I have to throw my autonomy away
to be with you, and as the fish
run scatter-stunned when the boat glides over them,
I am aware of my feelings wiggling like
snakes in the grass, waiting for an unwary passerby;
The boat docks in your world and complexity
threatens to strike
the granite-gray fences you have built
around your heart, unwilling to waltz
in the salt-marsh mud of emotion and conviction
because
you might get your white pants dirty——
only crabs can survive that mud
and crustaceans and reptiles
do not mix.

The Banquet

Loyalty has very thin skin, not unlike
the webs of moisture that form in early morning, only
to be
suffocated by the new sun. . . . .
Commerce was also invited to your feast, loading
his plate
with supply and demand potatoes;
Ethics grew fat on beef, but Holiness refused to saturate
her hunger, because she had learned the
discipline
of drawing the line between need and want. . . . .
Marriage arrived on the arm of Doughboy, a haunting
reminder
that commitment should not wed
the flaky dust of circumstance——
joy cannot take root in loose soil;
Nakedness showed up too in an attempt to spoil
the celebration by making sexuality a sin
instead of a way of letting God in;
The King ran him off, but he managed to pierce the flimsy
membranes
of Loyalty, Loneliness the ointment that was
applied to the
holes——
the wedding guests toasted the union
of life with death.

At the End of the Day

Now I lay me down to sleep,
not knowing if the climb to morning
will prove too steep. . . . .
I accept kisses from the dark,
hoping it will be light I embrace;
Steel moonbeams cast cold threats
across the still room
and I am afraid to sleep for
slaughter——
perhaps the new morning will last forever
and death will have been a friend
defeated as a foe. . . . .
There is no night there, you know,
and if my appointment arrives earlier than is the
custom,
how many more dawns than dusks
will I live to sow?

Epitaph

I had to love today,
because you couldn't promise me
tomorrow,
and my wealth is in the glimpse of the beyond
that escapes the indifferent eye,
flashing, twinkling in the tease of
sunlight
or the gray dewshine of raindrops. . . . .
I had to hold tightly to purpose,
because you might not give me time for
carelessness,
and lifeblood is too precious to spill on selfish
whim;
I had to cherish hope,
because you couldn't guarantee light
amid
despair, and I was tired of
hurting——
I am sustained by what I cannot see,
and reassured by a comforting grasp
that is all in all, ever powerful, ever good.
Because I was forced to live life boldly,
thankfully,
lovingly and
joyfully,
death is tender,
and life was a triumph.